# Jenny Mitchell

# Resurrection of a Black Man

## Indigo Dreams Publishing

First Edition: Resurrection of a Black Man
First published in Great Britain in 2022 by:
Indigo Dreams Publishing
24, Forest Houses
Cookworthy Moor
Halwill
Beaworthy
Devon
EX21 5UU

www.indigodreamspublishing.com

ISBN 978-1-912876-71-6

British Library Cataloguing in Publication Data. A CIP record
for this book can be obtained from the British Library.

Designed and typeset in Palatino Linotype by Indigo Dreams.
Cover design by Ronnie Goodyer from 'Portrait of Henry
Thomas, a Jamaican Man' by Glyn Philpot.

Printed and bound in Great Britain by 4edge Ltd.
Papers used by Indigo Dreams are recyclable products made
from wood grown in sustainable forests following the guidance
of the Forest Stewardship Council.

For my brother
Mark Anthony Mitchell

**Also by Jenny Mitchell**

*Her Lost Language, IDP, 2019*
*Map of a Plantation, IDP, 2021*

# Contents

100 Ways of Saying Black 8

**Sons**
Braiding 13
Barber off the Harrow Road 14
Black Rapunzel 15
brothers, 1970 16
Sestina for a Black Policeman 18
Black Men Carry Flowers 20
Song for Prison Island 21
Heavy Dub 22
Psalm 120 24

**Fathers**
Lowfields Jamaica 29
When We First Reach 30
Another Windrush Story 31
A History of Attacks 32
When Gollies Sell Like Hot Cakes 34
One Bright Morning 36
How to Grow an Orchid 38
Seven Stages of Dad 39
Late Flowering Dad 41

**Centaur**
animals 45
lights in every window 46
Hymn to Jamaica 47
Visiting a Giant with My Mother 48
On a Jamaican Road 49
Three Eyes Reading 50
He Crawls Through Words 52
Last Words 54
Centaur 55

**Resurrection of a Black Man**
He Looks Like Nat King Cole                60
He Wore a Yellow Crown                     62
Missing From the News Report               64
A Man in Love with Flowers                 66
Self-Portrait                              67
A Grand Piano in Jamaica, 1953             68
Old-time Movie Stars                       70
Library of Bats                            72
Resurrection of a Black Man                74

# Resurrection of a Black Man

# 100 Ways of Saying Black

| | | |
|---|---|---|
| Active | Aggressive | Angry |
| Animalistic | Ape | Asylum Seeker |
| Atavistic | Baboon | |

BAME (although whites are the global minority)

| | | |
|---|---|---|
| Barbarian | Beast | Belligerent |
| Berry | Blunt | Bronzed |
| Brown | Brown Sugar | Buck |
| Burden | Chalky White | |

*charming, wide-grinning piccaninnies* (Enoch Powell, 1968)

| | | |
|---|---|---|
| Chocolate | Cocky | Coco |
| Coconut | Coffee | Coco |
| Coon | Damned | Descendant of slaves |
| Devil | Diseased | Disadvantaged |
| Dusky | Ebullient | Energetic |
| Ethnic | Exuberant | Fierce |
| Foreign | Golliwog | Good dancer |
| Good at sport | Gun-wielding | Half-breed |
| Half-caste | Half-white | *Having a touch* |
| High spirited | High yellow | Hoodie |
| Illegal | Immigrant | Jungle bunny |
| Lazy | Lively | Mammy |
| Midnight | Mixed-race | Monkey |
| Mugger | Multicultural | Multi-ethnic |
| Mustee | Mustaphino | Nig |
| Nigger | Nig-nog | Non-white |
| *Not one of us* | Nuisance | Octoroon |
| *One of them* | Other | *Part of the fabric* |
| Physical | Primitive | Quadroon |
| Red | Refugee | Sable |
| Sambo | Scourge | Slick |
| *Some of my best friends* | | *Surprisingly* (insert at will) |
| *Sweet* (when young) | | Tan |
| Tar baby | Thin-skinned | Trick baby |

Twilight　　　　　　Unfortunate　　Vicious
Victim　　　　　　　Vivacious　　　Volatile
Wicked　　　　　　　Windrush Generation
Workshy　　　　　　...

# Sons

## Braiding

I place the comb against his scalp,
my son – a big man – legs spread
on the carpet. Red hibiscus shines –
the council flat my lost Jamaican yard.

He nudges close, firm shoulders pressed
between my knees like girls back home,
hair braided in the sun. Points
in pain towards his head. I take more time

to part the new-turned soil
as he begins – police again,
how hard their hands, the failure
to apologise that always ends this tale.

Beneath the words, I dream of fireflies,
their beat against the windowpane
as if locked out
is not the same as free.

When cane row is complete, he nods,
stands up, strolls to the door.
I'm never sure of his return.

## Barber off the Harrow Road

It's close to a black church, on hallowed ground –
ungentrified – no artisans, no pre-loved signs –
FOR SALE nailed to a cross along the narrow street, free
from traffic noise, the rush of crowds. This barber shop
is brightly lit, stained, glass panel in the door, new
coat of paint to hide the scrawl *Black Lives Out!*

Beyond the threshold, icons are worn photographs
placed on the walls with care – black men and boys
gazing up, angelic models with sharp cuts, afros standing
tall – a black power sign or dark, full moons. Rising
from the radio – *Wholly Holy* sang by Marvin Gaye –
*We proclaim love our salvation.*

Three red chairs in a row are thrones, three mirrors
smudged, three sinks, hair-flecked. The barber-god
is black, robe white, unhurried walk, pate shining
with a halo's glare – harsh florescent light. He points,
imperious, telling me to sit – not a roaring voice – soft
Jamaican lilt. My head soon in his hands, the ache is gone.

Palms gentle on warm scalp, I feel his breath as mine
until a towel's grabbed, fanned out, draped around
my neck. The world is tilted back. I'm lowered
to the sink's smooth edge. Water flows, hair baptised,
hard fingers give their best massage. Soap suds
are flicked so tenderly, to keep the sting from eyes.

I cry to feel this calm but make no sound except to hum
what I recall of Marvin's song, become my prayer –
*We should believe in one another. People,*
*we have got to come together.* More
hate crime spills out of the radio as I stand up, feel new
strength in my sharp cut. Each strand has its own spine.

## Black Rapunzel

Family gathers in these plaits,
each parting like a grave
for people forced to work
the cane, colour of my scalp,
sun beating on their crowns.

I'll twist the strands into a rope,
de-colonising hair, a diaspora
wending back to help
the ones in chains
escape the transatlantic.

Black Rapunzel, I'll uncoil my locks
in prison yards, urge those on SUS
or sectioned, deep ancestor
voices trapped in too-loose plaits,
to shimmy over walls,

hide beneath my headwrap – floral
length of Africa before the trade.
I'll carry them to safety
woven in my braids. We'll grieve
till loss flies out, unbound at last.

## brothers, 1970

they were coloured. then. it was nig-nog
from the blank men. on the small screen
where a comic spoke. of a golliwog
who goes in a pub. has his head bashed.
what a great laugh. as the nf march
the high street. enoch powell says
will turn dark red. when blacks move in
make the road shit. send them all back
to the jungle. but the young ones
call this home

brothers are close. in a grey block
where a black man. calls the whites blank
as they curse him. in the workplace
till he comes home. as a big man
with a thick belt. round his fat fist
hits the young ones. see the smallest
get a sharp lick. forced to stand back
when the big man. beats the oldest
as the sun glints. as the buckle lands
on the soft skin. once again

boys are best friends. but they can't run
when attack builds. or the big belt
will hit hardest. as the big man's growing
sky high. he is fee-fi. he is fo-fum
as he spills blood. like the blank men
beat the slaves. so the young boys
beg to be saved. they are not heard
they are enraged. they are in rage
as one falls down. tries to hold on
he is mum's yoke. when she stands by

as the black man. wends a big belt
but the youngest. knows to get out
on a full grant. when he's eighteen
barely six months. till a duppy lands
on his brother's throat. he dies in his sleep
there is no cause. not yet twenty-one
what a quiet end. for a quiet man
with the best laugh. from the deep dark
where his pain grew. in this cold land
he called home

## Sestina for a Black Policeman

It happens near a bridge, some steps before it flows
across the river Thames – both lanes blocked. A cordon
indicates an accident or crime. I only see him –
the black cop – when two white men ram in his back.
He turns, teeth bared, arms raised against a human tide
that's risen up to overwhelm without much warning.

A wave of noise erupts when he hurls out a warning,
louder than a sea wall falling. With a punch, the flow
of people stop to turn and point, form a restless tide,
staring at the unfair fight moving closer to the cordon.
Police run up and down, shoving people back,
as one black man dredges up power deep inside of him.

The two attackers punch with force, mean to knock him
down, a resolute attack that he resists, forewarned –
there is no doubt – by forebears who dwell in his back,
rising up if danger comes too close. His body flows
out of the way, protected by a tough ancestor cordon,
standing firm against the sudden surge, a rushing tide.

Two white men look surprised to find there is a tide
of strength in one black cop; curse to weaken him.
The n-word calls more forebears to the cordon.
Those who died enslaved, yelling out a warning,
push with all their might as they once pushed the flow,
hurled from a slaving ship, unable to swim back.

He does not know what comes to life inside his back.
Africa – the entire continent – moves in him like a tide
that means he has great stamina, though blood flows
from a wound as both attackers punch again, kick him
to the ground. He slips, stands up, calls out a warning:
*There is no escape. Each step leads to the cordon.*

The two attackers hunker down to push into the cordon
of one black man whose colleagues watch, standing back
when he's kneed in the groin, gritted teeth a warning –
he's struggling to hold his own against the human tide
much longer. Both assailants lift their feet, knock him
to the ground, but more ancestors offer strength that flows.

They stand strong as the cordon, flexible enough to flow
into his limbs, their warning cry so loud, a swelling tide
inside his back, rising up, an inner force protecting him.

## Black Men Carry Flowers

red blossoms on their palms. hibiscus
blooms from fingertips. waterlilies circle
wrists in contrast to their shade
                              heavy-laden
with this crop, they move with grace. vines
cling to arms. ferns worn as green insignia.
warriors of peace
                              they grow
on any street. if you look up. see men are grand
estates. a wealth of plants. once torn
from land. they burgeon in the wild
                              reach out
in dappled light. wide shoulder blades replete
with yellow orchids. chests are dappled lawns
rolling to a bank of leaves
                              delicate but strong
morning glories shape their legs. bougainvillea
bends the knees. ripples as it clings to thighs
tumbling to the shins.
                              agile on the ground
jasmine moves the feet. every step a heady scent
rising through a man-made-plant. flourishing.
their words fall out as petals.

## Song for Prison Island

In Zanzibar, the giant turtles clack together as they mate,
crashed spaceships tilting with the impact
as the one beneath urges forward to escape.

I watch behind a fence, next to a German tourist
with her mixed-race son. He hurries up and down,
aims a stick through bars to poke at the soft heads.

His mother stands, green eyes averted.
Does she even hear him scream: *Make the nasty stop.*
Being black, I sense the tourists long before they speak:

*Look. That's typical.* He charges at the fence again,
the stick a lethal weapon, voice a madman's threat:
*Make the nasty stop.* Turtles pull apart. I hear:

*He's running wild. They can't be controlled.*
The boy now grips the fence, shaking to the roots,
raving with a need to run in all directions.

I whisper to his crown: *The turtle's going to eat
the little boy.* His fists release their hold as he repeats:
*The turtle's going to eat the little boy.*

## Heavy Dub

Jamaicans them is funny people –
give out nicknames like a real name is a coin,
could be stolen any time. Children were. Land. Religion.

Mummy says her Lloydie's mind is taken up
with slavery days. *Why, when he was born in England?*

Doctors only have two words from him – *Jungle Boy*
like friends hailed out at school.
Couldn't stand his given name – Lloyd Winston Campbell.
Cried when watching Roots –
*Where's my Kunte Kinte?*

Now in hospital, mummy slides her eyes away from him,
barely moving on the bed,
towards the *red-skinned bitch*
holding hands with what *could be* his daughter,
orange ribbons in *good hair.*

They cling together when the nurse checks on the tubes
lodged down his throat. Choking sound.
As a choir boy, he caused such gladness in the church –
Head thrown back. Buck teeth. A soaring voice.
*Who will roll away the stone?*

Tall for nine, weighed
down with *Why did daddy have to leave?*
as if a council flat could hold – *I must be free.*

Jungle Boy would not be good for anyone.
Laughed too loud in class. Detained.
Forced to scrawl a hundred lines.
Mummy used a belt against bare legs.

Jungle Man or Natty Dread refused to find a job.
Studied books on slavery days, captive in a fog of spliff.
Called all white men *Babylon*.

Mummy kicked him out,
had enough to deal with
trapped behind a till all day.

Natty with his hair unwashed,
moved in with the red-skinned girl.
She left when the baby came.

He inhaled his feelings with the skunk,
skanking in the street to heavy dub –
loud, insistent traffic noises –
shouting at the sky –
*I am a frangipani tree!*

Sectioned. Cuffed.
Knee pressed in his lower back.
Released when lithium – that soothing punch –
levelled him
like cutting down a tree to praise the stump.

Yesterday – grey beard, locs thin – he balanced one foot
off the curb. No one heard him say *I'll skank*
*to my true Mother Country.*

Driver only saw a flash.
Mummy hears her Lloydie gag.
Red-skin and her daughter wail.
Nurse pulls up the sheet, steps back.
*Who will roll away the stone?*

## Psalm 120

*I am for peace but when I speak, they are for war*
is quoted on my father's fist – the right – in tiny script
we could not read until his death, laid on a page – white
cotton sheet – his bed become a book recounting thoughts
he hid, refusing to come close or open up although
our house was cramped. Now it expands, the fist released,
breath ebbing back. Strange flow of blood reveals a palm
he did not offer us – no holding hands – sharp slaps.
His parchment skin says this, 'I will speak the truth. Can't
be blamed for my own life, forced to bear each quote.'

The left hand tells this tale – 'My dad was bible-chained,
agile with a cane. He scarred my skin.' Around the wrist –
*My soul hath dwelt with him that hated peace.* A muscled
forearm says, 'I beat your mother up, wounds hidden
under clothes. She passed with drink. I said she left. You
took the blame, and I agreed. Who'd want a boy
that cried?' Shoulders shrug, reveal this quote, *Woe is me,*
*that I sojourn in Mesech, that I dwell in the tents of Kedar.*
I have to google it, bereft of clues until I read Kedar's
a nomad tribe. He gambled us from one dump to the next.

His chest, once strong as oak, bears a wealth of scars –
doctors searched to find a heart. Did they stamp this quote –
*Sharp arrows of the mighty, with coals of juniper?*
I look it up: God punishes the sinner with severity.
Does that mean dad or me for challenging his flaws, more
than skin deep? I want to know when my mum died, attack
the trembling corpse – say this instead, 'I will accept him
as he was.' Look back to see a scrawl upon his chin –
*What shall be given unto thee? or what shall be done*
*unto thee, thou false tongue?*

His mouth moves fast – 'I only hurt those who hurt me.'
Words blush across his cheeks: *Deliver my soul, O Lord,*
*from lying lips, and a deceitful tongue.* There's more:
*In my distress, I cried unto the Lord, and he heard me.*
I shout, 'Liar,' at his face, would not have dared when
he could punch. The air begins to change, thick with his
weeping for the first time. I slip to hear, 'My son,
how can I rest till you forgive?' Impossible to trust this
voice, I google once again: Each verse calls for ascent.
He levitates, jaw slack, recites the psalm, start to end.

# Fathers

## Lowfields, Jamaica

A thinning man in a hospice bed
has to use his whole frame, his whole mind
to answer the question, *Where do you live?*
Slowly he says, *Lowfields, Jamaica.*

I know he's lived in England for over fifty years.
He came as a boy who helped his father
gather the cane. It blooms on the top
when it's time to cut down, so he tells me.

I hear a rattling sound when he speaks –
the duppies have taken his lungs. He remembers
the time he dared his kid brother to climb
on the roof of the Colony Club, reserved for the whites.

He unhooked the Union Jack and waved it
above his head in triumph.
The constable beat him into the jail,
beat him till his eyes were closed.

His left arm was never the same again.
He refused to sing *God Save the Queen*
in school after that and was caned for refusing.
Lowfields, Jamaica – yes.

He came as a boy who helped his father
gather the cane. It blooms on the top
when it's time to cut down, so he tells me.
It blooms on the top when it's time to cut down.

## When We First Reach

The whites them used to say we colours was too bright.
You couldn't trust a darkie in a yellow suit – too sharp.
Him steal your wife with one hand,
pick your pocket with the next.

Them never think to say we dress up bright
to keep the sun alive in this dull place. I never know
a sky so grey or clouds this low till I did buck up here.
The whites them wear their clothes to match,

heads bent like words drop from their mouths.
They read them off the ground, mumbling to themselves.
Is not unfriendly them unfriendly.
Is just the cold did lick them

till they can't do little more than frown,
faces long like icicles. Another thing them used to say,
we eat dog food. Why dog food? Why not cat?
You ever hear such foolishness? Enough to make me spit.

The young ones tell me rest myself. Is not the past
we living now. You go to Carnival and all you see is whites
eat jerk food, dress up bright.
But me? I see a next thing come to pass –

these days is all we blacks who wear dull clothes.
Is progress this
or something sad we catch?

## Another Windrush Story

Daddy dressed in expectations,
high-steps off the ship, afraid
of nothing but the foggy shape
of Britain on his breath,
smiling as if God cried *Cheese!*

The grin is not returned
by men in hunching overcoats.
Doors slammed in his face,
he finds an attic room,
carpeted with mice.

Hardly space to hang
a bus conductor's uniform, boots
like boulders running up and down
to take the fares. Shamed
by men who call him *Boy*.

Women reach to touch his tail.
Tell their children *Don't be scared.*
*Rub a nigger's head for luck.*
Daddy does not bend or curse.
Saves up for a terrace house.

Welcomed to the neighbourhood
by spit hacked at the door.
But he smiles in photographs,
to impress the folks back home.
God cries *Cheese*!

## A History of Attacks

The first against my uncle when a child
around his age but white, stopped him on the road
to Kingston town. Perhaps it was torn clothes,
no seat to hand-me-downs my uncle wore
when young that made the child send out a fist.
My uncle says it was a manly punch.

It seemed to mark him out, that single punch,
as even though he grew in height, another child,
this time at school – a wooden shack – used fists
to knock my uncle down, climbed on his back, rode
like a horse. Long trousers were soon frayed.
His dad beat him for spoiling the new clothes.

In time, my uncle trained to be a tailor. Clothes
meant more to him than friends. He almost thumped
a stranger who stroked a brocade coat worn
to a dance, my uncle's coming out – such child-like
glee to join the Commonwealth. He led the way –
a wild conga – till the touch, his body a clenched fist.

Coming to the mother country, cold felt like a fist
right in the face. My uncle says his clothes
were too thin for the house, much less icy streets.
Friends from the US, black queens, made hot punch
at Christmas time, given as a gift. One said *Child,*
*you have to learn to hold your drink. Be warned.*

He meant the Teddy Boys who roamed, wore
suits to fascinate my uncle but used fists
to knock blacks into the next week like children
being punished by a dad. My uncle's clothes
contained bright sun, made him a target for a punch.
When drunk, he staggered in the road.

But having been attacked out in the road
too many times to count on both his hands, he wore
a knuckle duster, kept that metal punch
deep inside a pocket, firmly on his fist.
One young Ted yelled *Poof* pointing at the clothes,
bore down to beat my uncle as if he was a child.

He scanned the open road, ran at the youth,
began to curse, punched with his shielded fist,
wore out a face, took a breath, fixed up his clothes.

## When Gollies Sell Like Hot Cakes

We trail him through the fenced-in bombsite, kicking
down his name – *Babatunde* aimed towards a map
of holes in drooping socks, stain the shape of Africa
across the seat of ragged pants. We sing this loud –
*Tar Baby. Babatunde's wet himself again.* He shakes
his head – pity I can't understand at the age of twelve,
dumped in a care home. He's the only black.

We're taught by men attached to walking sticks,
leftovers from the war; women with dead loves chained
around thin necks, saying the new queen's *A saint*
married to a *Naval God* – Prince Philip as a Boy's Own
dream – father who is always strong. I tell myself
that mine – unknown – is lost in Africa, *Invaded
by the Wops*, a teacher shouts. *Saved by our brave lads.*

Now in peace, the Wogs set fire to the Union Jack.
They'd kill the mothers we have never met or just
recall – the heady scent of talc, quick hug before the door
slams shut. We sing until it rhymes – *Babatunde
cannot use a knife and fork.* Add *Nig-nog* when
he doesn't cry. At night, the boy's dorm shakes
with tears, snot captured on worn pillow cases.

The next day during prayers, Babatunde's called up
to the front. We want to see him caned for nothing
more than playing on his own beside the swings,
counting stones into a pile as we shoot guns made
by our hands, like heroes in the films, to kill the Wogs,
the Wops, the Indians although Nurse Shan gives out
sweets, sings *You're so brave* dealing with the nits.

Babatunde is not caned when he goes to the front.
A blue-black soldier near the Head calls out *My son*.
Arms wide, he pulls the boy into his chest. I want
to be called *Babatunde* in a voice that's rich and dark
as Bovril or the Aga Khan. At night, I dream an African
looks at my ragged clothes, shakes his head until
the teachers lower theirs, lifts me up, takes me home.

## One Bright Morning

It's happening today – a soon-to-be offender sneers,
points towards the only black boy in his class,
sends out a curse, aimed many times at the television
by his dad, flag held high when *One of them* appears,
sad-faced on a fragile boat, drifting out to sea.
*Drown them all at birth*, his father shouts.

*Go back where you belong*, his loyal son shouts
towards the new boy, fists about to strike, sneering
in the playground, urged on by his friends, a sea
of large white lads, most of whom nod off in class.
They feel such strength, puffed up, when it appears
to agitate the teachers, as if they are a gang on television.

The playground has become a scene on television,
where the new boy's chased, hunted down, shouting
out for help, arms raised, though not to fight – he appears
to drown. Cut to another scene – a coastguard sneers
when a boat tips in high waves, the loss of life classed
as a risk *These people* take by challenging the sea.

Back to the boy who's been engulfed, lost in a sea
of fists, feet aimed towards his head. On the television,
a gang might cheer to see the blood, but this rowdy class
of boys-turned-into-thugs steps back. One shouts.
*Leave him alone* – too late. The injured child sneers
with a rictus grin, hand salvaging his heart, so it appears.

No one breathes in the playground till they all appear –
teachers running for the young boy's life. A rushing sea
of them push back the gang, stare at the sneering
mask, a knife deep in the chest like on the television,
blade drowned up to the hilt. A teacher shouts,
*Move back*, herds the gang towards its class.

They can't be contained as members of their class
call out, point towards one running boy. He appears
to be the owner of the knife. *No!* His father shouts
at the police. *It's not his fault. Blame the bloody sea
of refugees who swamp our land.* He's seen on television,
thrown into a van, as is his son, the same loyal sneer.

They're called a *Symbol of their class* with a sneer,
as if they shout the headlines, send out a constant sea
of blame till refugees appear as enemies on television.

## How to Grow an Orchid

He marches in at first, back straight, left, right.
Pulls the spare room on his shoulders, heavy
as a trench coat. Hunkers
in an armchair. Reads a barrage
of bad news: *World Teeters on the Brink.*
Followed by the football scores.

His wife, through quaking walls, is bomb.
Baby's cry – a siren.
Hard to hear without his squad –
ease of men about to die,
watch the same in someone else.
Breast milk makes him think of blood.

After that, he hurries with the radio,
dial turned up. Clicks the lock.
Listens for more casualties.
How to grow an orchid. Bach
had twenty children. Did they clench
their fists, threaten hand-to-hand?

The girl shouts *Daddy* at the door.
All doors are daddy now. He blocks
his ears against her scream. Ache
in his jaw. Tomorrow – outlook bright.
Manly voice of hope. He won't look down.
*But, Jesus, wrists are hard to cut.*

## Seven Stages of Dad

Beginning with his death will make this safe,
that's what I tell the page, knowing I can't stop,
even if he rises from the ground, resurrects
his bulk on every line, fists clenched, lips
clamped until he shouts, *You must not speak!*
Those were the words he hurled at me.

Not that he ever spoke that much to me,
huddled in a corner of my body. I felt safe
towards the end, him struggling to speak,
cancer deep inside his throat, a harsh full stop
placed on his right to shout. In dreams, his lips
move fast – *I have the strength to resurrect.*

Why not? He acted like a god – they resurrect,
death a minor obstacle. I know he'd knocked me
down to hear these words, smother with his lips
pressed into mine, used like a wife. Not safe
to tell you more – details may cause alarm. I'll stop
at this – his zip undone, hand on my arm. *Don't speak.*

As if I have the words for what's unspeakable,
me crushed beneath his weight when he resurrects,
an ache shoved deep inside my back. It only stops
if I cry out, *It hurts too much!* My God, he's haunting me,
crawling under skin, whispering in veins, *Not safe
to tell a word of this,* although words burn my lips.

Standing near his coffin was the same. My lips
felt hot, blistered every time I tried to speak,
say dirt must hold him down to keep me safe,
in the hope that he – a devil – could not resurrect,
walk on holy ground. Still, he feels so close to me,
his voice held in the graveyard trees. *Stop!*

That word lands with autumnal leaves. *Stop!*
It rises up, a bitter breeze that chaffs my lips
as I call out, *He's here!* The mourners stare at me,
pat my arm, say I mustn't grieve so hard, speak
softly in my ear. They do not see him resurrect,
kick at dirt, a devil's grin to show I am not safe.

He tells me *Stop!* again. Now mourners are not safe.
I yell, *There is no way to silence me. I shall speak.*
Truth falls out of my lips to blight his resurrection.

## Late Flowering Dad

It grows out of his grave, the love
he never showed becomes the grass, green
breath thick on the ground, a field
with each embrace – once held back,
now rife. A tree grows tall for every slap.

The forest looks so dark until an alchemy
of hugs hangs loose from every branch.
Pluck them down, hold to the heart, breathe
to know death does not end. His life
becomes my path, a way to thrive.

# Centaur

**animals**

Grandfather tramped through childhood / barefoot stealing food / green-gold bananas from a neighbour's field / all lizard when he scaled the wall / monkey-limbed / he grabbed the fruit / placed it in his shirt / close to his heart / all crow / flew along a burning road / ignited / by a high jamaican sun / smiled to think of slowing down to peel the unripe skin / heard a distant growl / english mastiff / hurled / its body / weapon / close / not the rage of teeth against bare legs / grandfather said / but the drip / of thick saliva running down his sole / woke him up / in ditches late at night / when he built a three-room shack / big dogs made him back away / puppies saw him reach for stones / he became all mastiff / then

## lights in every window

grandfather drives her out that night. looms height. and rum-inflated weight. walks grandmother down. the steps of a three-room shack. both young. in what they'll call the golden times her backwards. mouthing *no*. neighbours must not hear. *no* said again. it makes him raise his fist. to block out light. except pink dots. beneath her lids. she sprawls across the ground. he spits towards this woman who will bear. twelve children. four buried in the yard. he slams the door. a lamp shakes dizzy. in the window he moves towards another drink. she crawls into their car. rust-filled. a missing wheel. insects nestle in the seats crackle underfoot. windows glisten. with the light. a low half-moon. she sits proud. in the driver's seat. hands on the steering wheel. *go*. cracks an insect. underneath her foot. *drive*. says a windowpane. even if she could. this three-legged beast would not go far. she sees bright dots ahead. leading to a house. she wants to call her own. lights in every window. but it is a cat lazing on the path. eyes bright enough to lead this woman. to another town. she hums. a steady engine sound. sings about the dawn. *i watch. the sunlight. shine through clouds.* her voice is soft and low. *i watch the sunset fade.* the cat moves on. wide stretch beyond the path. grandmother huddles down. grandfather opens up the door. calls her name. a light on in the neighbour's house. grandfather calls again. she is a dog. must obey. go to a man. she hardly knows. will never know. the sun begins to rise

# Hymn to Jamaica

*'We are going home rejoicing / where Our Father's dwelling stands.'*

Granny's coffin stands as if a spine has met the grain,
open to her life-sized portrait decomposing in the heat –
corrugated shack: a boiling pot; lid – sun-buckled roof.

Even dead, propped against a corner to save space,
she can sense grandfather slump back on a sagging chair.
Knows he will not buy a stone carved with her name.

It would cost a week of pay when he never works
two days in a row without the need to rest, recuperate.
Rum is medicine of choice. Falling down another cure.

He's sick enough to let her rot so he will not be alone.
Arms-crossed, she calls the spirit-soul, strength beyond
mere breath – to rouse my mother in our Kilburn flat.

She shivers with the cold, blinks in the light. Flies
a plane towards an inch of yard-made-landing strip.
Ignores the weeping on the chair. Nails the coffin down.

Shoulders to a plot. Shovels dirt. Chisels stone – granny's name
along with her three titles: Wife, Mother, Drudge.
A hymn seeps from the mound – *I am going home rejoicing.*

## Visiting a Giant with My Mother

We fly towards the damp unsettling heat of Jamaica,
where a dazzling light makes the runway shimmer,
like an uncontrolled flame travelling out before me,
eyes open wide, startled by this strange new landscape,

where a dazzling light makes the runway shimmer
till appearing to totally melt the giant airport. Doors
open wide. Startled by a strange new landscape,
I ask my mother to describe her father again. *Will he cry*

*till appearing to totally melt?* The giant airport doors
close behind us. Hawkers bear down as we try to hail
a cab. I ask her to describe her father again. *Will he cry*
*to see you after all these years, or are feelings kept*

*close?* Behind us, hawkers bear down. As we try to hail
a cab, they demand money. Everyone looks strange.
I ask, *Will he be glad to see us both?* Her irritation, usually kept in
check, is suddenly released, both hands clenched.

Hawkers demand money. Every one of them looks strange, but
she seems mad, voice raised after a lifetime
spent mumbling. She pushes back, both fists clenched.
It's what he would do, the father she calls a towering lush.

Now the hawkers stand back as she pushes me towards
a cab, screaming as if we're caught up in some sort of riot.
That's what he would do, the father she calls a towering lush
would say *Let's go to the nearest bar to get drunk,*

*till we're caught in some sort of riot.* She laughs, pretends it's a
joke as I help her into a cab. I laugh too as she says, *If we were*
*in England, I'd take you to a pub to get drunk until we fly*
*towards the damp unsettling heat of Jamaica.*

## On a Jamaican Road

The driver leaves us all to suffer with the heat
inside the rust-baked country bus.
Runs towards the water falling
foaming from between two giant rocks.

He throws aside his shirt, kicks off his boots,
keeps his trousers on. The battered hat
stands high – pushed back
by long, escaping dreads.

As soon as he steps in the water,
his darkly-muscled back turns slick.
Chin down, he offers up a prayer
until the fall becomes a Cross

between two mighty boulders. Water is a crystal,
melting colours of the sun – so luminous,
the sound – a fright of duppies
calling to themselves.

The man turns round, whips off his hat,
shakes. Shards of water rent the air,
black diamonds nestle in his dreads,
opaque pearls light up his skin.

His hat becomes a bowl. He tips the water
on his head, nods to the sun, picks up
the shirt, the boots. Strolls to the bus
and loud complaints.

He shrugs, resumes his seat,
drives past stagnant streams,
broken fences, people slaving in the fields.

### Three Eyes Reading

My father only has one seeing eye, the left
boxed blind – a drunken accident grandfather
says was no one's fault. The punch helped calm
him down. Beating children made him smile,
especially his youngest sons – a set of twins:
Dad and an uncle bullied for their gentleness.

Three older sons were anything but gentle,
so keen to fight in the playground, they left
a trail of blood up to the swings. My father
ran away from other boys who chased his twin
as well. Both targets for revenge stayed calm
when cornered. Bloody noses made them smile.

Their widowed father beat them more, smiling
with each blow, meant to thump all tenderness
out of their *weakling selves*. They stayed calm,
never cried despite a belt, as if the loss of that left
eye drained their tear ducts, the brothers twinned
in stoic strength to face an enraged father.

He began to spoil his three *hard lads*, a father
who applauded fights, wore a beaming smile
at rotten school reports – not for the twins –
both praised as kind and studious, a gentle
force for good who helped out in the library, left
shelves neat, choosing books to read in peace.

They did so in the unkempt garden, no peace
inside the house. When it was dark, their father
called them in to cook him *Something nice*, left
them scraps. Reeling from the pub, he smiled,
determined to beat up the boys – *Those gentlemen*,
he growled. *Three Eyes Reading. Useless twins.*

He ate the well-cooked food, beat up the twins,
claiming meat was raw, potatoes hard. They calmly
tended wounds, then stood upright like gentlemen,
to ask three rowdy brothers and a glaring father
if they wanted more. My dad knew that a smile
would make the hard men upturn chairs and leave.

The twins were safe alone inside the house, left
to raise their gentle voices briefly, cursed their father
who returned to calm. Three Eyes Reading smiled.

## He Crawls Through Words

Here are a few my father makes me dwell upon,
now speech and breath are lost to him – prostrate –
not stretched out in submission or in adoration –
the first of several definitions I cannot accept.
No, he lay overcome most days, done in by drink,
not working much except to pay for booze, the rent.

A city lad – one of six born out of wedlock. The rent
was paid in coins found in unwashed clothes, placed on
a landlord's palm with a *Hail Mary*. Granny drank
herself to sleep, relief my father says, prostrate
with it, surprised because the shortfall was accepted.
When sober, she knelt down to show God adoration.

It's another word my father calls to mind – adoration –
worship, veneration – though it is too much. I did not rent
my clothes to find him dead but shrugged, accepted
he had taken breath for longer than I'd hoped, frail on
the bed, shrunk down in size towards the end. Prostrate
means drained as well, not of blood but by drink.

His face was etched with careful lines from all the drink
he'd ever taken, as if skin showed weird adoration
for spirits, also known as ghosts. Was he prostrate
at times because life haunted him? Yes, he paid the rent,
wore clean clothes, but frittered meagre savings on
rounds for his fast friends. Was it a bid to be accepted?

The opposite helps bring him back to life – *unaccepted*.
I turned away from his hunched frame many times, drunk
in the street, reeling in his hard-pressed suit, walking on
the side of polished shoes. It took some time for adoration
to be transformed, the child I was – keen to forgive – rent
in half, able to walk past him near a pub, even if prostrate.

Still, it came as a surprise to learn about the prostrate
cancer, only fifty-five years old. Much harder to accept
he shunned all medication, even when he knew it rent
my heart to see him sick, finding ways of hiding drink,
installed in my spare room. Those nights he lay upon
the bed, calling out for help, tears fell with adoration.

Prostrate with it at times, I loved to hear how he adored
my mum, rent in half when she died young of drink.
Hard to accept she left no words for me to dwell upon.

## Last Words

They came out on his death
laid on a cooling board – rough cedar
plank with holes, allowing blood and waste
to drip through a white shroud
onto a bed of ice. Melting pink,
it slowed the rot.

The morgue attendant said it must have been the breeze.
A dead man could not say *I love,*
cloth tight around his jaw. Five sons insisted,
they did not want the lips to part,
believing in the old wives' tale –
a ghost escapes from any hole.

They argued for a while, agreed
their father rarely talked, preferring to wield canes.
How could he speak in death,
to be so sentimental?
He never mentioned love,
not even to his wife.

The voice was heard again,
coming from the ruined face,
eyes so deep they might have been pushed in
by angry thumbs, chin still proud,
which seemed a cheek –
the cloth was soiled.

His children hurried to the door
as it was said again – *I love,*
faint as a breeze but certain.

# Centaur

He ran       through all the fields       Grandfather

    Black stallion       Moon       rising

from hard flanks       Sun shone       to glimpse his smile

    Dark clouds    across       a troubled brow

Almighty hooves       trod    enemies to dust

    Proud       Muscular    Too tall

for any roof    He battered    gates       Kicked over

    fences       Felled    his wife

and other women       Fathered all the children

       longing for a chance

to ride upon his back       survey the world

    made at his height    dazzled    by his mane

Strong neck       pulsating       with all life

    Our Hero       Patriarch

No death       A further field

# Resurrection
## of a Black Man

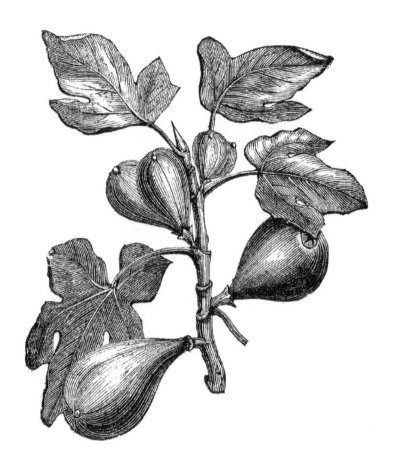

*A fig tree calls him father*

## He Looks Like Nat King Cole

Uncle Sidney glides out of a song – *Smile*
*though your heart is aching.* Black man
in a golden suit he makes himself, precisely
the same shade as covers on his three-piece suite.
Tassels are a give-away. He looks at men too much,
can't decide which queen he loves the most –
Bette Davis bites off words, strides down stairs,
Joan Crawford with her blood-red fingernails.

Blood pools in his shoes before the flames
set fire to hibiscus trees in his Jamaican yard,
hills running to a stream. My family is too prim
to talk about the end, his body battered, charred.
For now, he strides upstairs, an ornate flat
in Maida Vale, rose splendour of shag carpet
laid throughout. No men ever sleep the night.
His sewing kit is neat, shaped like a music box –

*One day my prince will come.* Pins prick
a velvet frog from Liberty – the first black man
to cut their cloth in '58. Proud to wear the uniform,
exchanged for a gold watch. Begins to dye
his hair at sixty-five, wear a brocade coat.
Police are called – a cottage in the Harrow Road.
My family call him *spinster aunt.* He flies back
to his *Island in the sun* – a rotting bungalow.

Flamboyant trees bow to a field of orchids.
He joins the Pentecostal church, cooking
for a cautious priest, *Sidney* murmured
like a prayer. On his way home, sun dying flame,
men stagger from a tin shebeen, sing *Batty man, bye-bye,*
force him in his home, knock him down,
a fire set to laugh at flames. The roof gives way.
My uncle screams – *The sun comes shining through.*

## He Wore a Yellow Crown

My uncle's golden suit lies on his bed,
abandoned treasure with wide shoulder blades,
spread on a field of plush pink candlewick,
the floors all cleaned of blood, as is the house,
a week after he's killed, crushed by a gang.

Look at the dazzling weave. He sewed by hand,
large mitts made delicate to touch a bolt of light
from Liberty. It shines with King-like grace,
warmed his chest to brave cold English
streets. Sharp seams retain no sign of broken bones.

Cloth does not scream for help the way he did,
or cry that he was *fully gay*. He called himself,
*No longer young but never old*. Still went in search
at night for what he termed his *special friends*.
Recalled their names as boots stamped on his spine.

I have been told he learned to strut when young,
swished off the boat that sailed him from Jamaica,
rouge upon his cheeks. For the first time,
my family could not call him *spinster aunt*.
The gang yelled to his roof *Batty man, bye bye*.

He loved to wear a yellow cap set at a slant,
bass sang *A hat's not a hat till it's tilted*. Style
led him to call men *she* or *her* when they attacked,
fighting back at times, too often in a hospital.
On that last night, he went straight to the morgue.

If beaten there were no complaints, though
he bemoaned the harm to self-made clothes,
hated names like bent, old queen – *Less of the old,
if you please.* He waved a regal hand when spat upon.
The gang tore off his rings,

attacked the ornaments he placed with care,
kicked skirting from his frame, yelled *Goal!*
Aimed the yellow cap against four walls,
whilst firmly on his head.
Shouted *Scored!*

## Missing From the News Report

*Catch him! Hold him! Knock him down!*
Not a breeze. An arm swings out, hits
my uncle to the floor of his sitting room,
parquet tiles he shone with his own hands –
three-piece suite now stained with blood.

A gang broke down his door, having followed
on a path made uneven by a day bored
drinking. Cheering loud to cause him harm,
they shout up at his roof, *Batty man, bye bye!*
Blows land hard, feet aiming at his back.

Sharp pain rips through his neck the moment
when he screams *Help me, please!* Their fists
attack. *Dirty little bum boy!* Feet pummelling
his back, blood gushing from the nose,
running down to pool on crimson lips.

Here's the sound of tearing – skin
beneath his suit. *Batty man still breathing?*
With another punch, sight begins to fade,
walls forget their roots, tumble
to the floor, offering this gift – ground

he cleared of scrub when he first moved in,
making it an Eden, lies in front of him.
First, he mows the lawn. Then a season
waiting, sensitive to soil as he has been
to cloth, tailor since a child.

Here, he sees the plants – primrose
open to the sky. Jasmine with her will
to climb. Violet is a Venus plant. Chamomile,
those little suns, offer him their soothing
scent just before the end.

## A Man in Love with Plants

I'll start this by transforming his last words.
*Help me, please!* becomes *I have gone upon a mission.*
That's how my uncle spoke, each word precise,
although he did not have much
education, his childhood drab as dirt
assailed the floorboards of a leaning shack.

Outside his final house, he worships life
held in hibiscus buds, red as new-
spilt blood. Roses shade the path.
Yellow orchids make him beam,
jasmine does the same even when
a gang plucks his last breath.

He lies as if awake, feet aimed up at the ceiling,
hole gaping through his golden suit –
self-made, a tailor since a child
in love with floral cloth. I know
he'd seek more plants to bless
his garden-church beyond the house.

## Self-portrait

He does not wear his finest clothes, golden suit
he makes himself – protection from the English
cold – shirt in dazzling shades, Jamaican
garden growing on his chest.

Here he sports a simple top, medallions
from *special friends* – men he loved the most,
their locks of hair worn near his heart.
The backdrop's plain in contrast to his flat –

a golden, three-piece suite, objet d'art from Liberty,
a wealth of books – a stage of sorts, safe
haven from the streets. Here, no one calls him *Wog*.
He's never chased or spat upon.

The backdrop makes his features glow – dark
brown skin. Brown eyes stare straight ahead,
a man who's been attacked much more than once,
laid up in hospital. He always answered back,

except returning home – Jamaica – *Island
in the sun*. Stepping off the plane, heat stirred
a furnace. His father wasted final breaths –
*Here comes the sodomite, hell-bound.*

My uncle wore gold to the funeral, hibiscus
on the headstone, paid for by a *Loving Son*.
If you look close, its twin can just be seen half-
hidden in the portrait.

## A Grand Piano in Jamaica, 1953

My father's skin glows like the instrument,
both squat with massive frames. He's not as black –
burnt brown – life working in the sun. When night
falls on a humid day, the Grand is heaved inside
our shack, keys jangling to a thud. Space retracts,
an inch left in the parlour cramped with chairs, my bed,
old boots, clothes rolled into a corner. Furniture
can't breathe, squashed against the instrument;
photographs unhinged in frames. Walls fail to look
each other up and down. The lid is opened, wide
yawn revealing parts my father calls *The guts.*

He watches, chin held low, still sweating from a day
spent heaving bricks to build a church for whites.
My music teacher laughs into a pink cravat, pale
hand upon *The magic music box.* He points at me,
*How many coloured boys in rags can play as well?*
I'm meant to smile, pleased with the unexpected gift,
except my father's waist is flush against the Grand,
fists plonked as if to undermine its size. He growls
to see an outstretched hand, pink as the cravat. Released,
my teacher holds his fingers tight as they turn red.

Waving the uninjured hand, he leaves the shack, hurries
down the path, bordered by a failing crop, into a Triumph
van, three heaving black men in the back. He shouts,
*I'm going home to England for the Coronation but won't
forget the Grand I've left behind with you.* The sun drops
yellow bunting as the loud horn blares – *What a Friend
We Have in Jesus* – drowned out by my father's voice,
the Grand between us like a dream I'll never have again.
He shouts *This gift is shit. It won't pay the blasted rent.
Who told that man to speak of rags inside my house?*

He hurls himself towards me in the inch left by the Grand,
grips my ragged collar. *That scholarship will make you think
life isn't about work. I'll smash it up – the guts as well – unless
I get a decent price.* He leaves the shack as I play Mozart's
Requiem for Two – imagine Sir's long hands. My father
hurries back, shadowed by the English priest. They barter
till it's clear silver is the only thing they worship. Taken
to the church, the Grand becomes my distant dream – heard
never seen as even with a new queen on the throne, coloured
boys back then were banned from the white church.

## Old Time Movie Stars

My uncle learns to curse down by a stream,
rolls harsh words away, carries over rocks,
feeds to jumping fish. Jamaican sun beats
on his head as he stands firm to scream – a child
not more than twelve, skin smarting from attack.
It won't be safe to go home till it's dark.

His father is a sweat-stained labourer, working
in the sun to build a tin shebeen. A white boss owns
the still that keeps men in that town – perched on a hill,
blue as a bruise – from walking straight. They stink
of booze most nights, curse the road, hail the moon,
pick up sticks to lick their young.

My uncle cannot run from any beating, to dare
will make them worse. He has to bear the switch
across his back in hand-me-downs – his brother's shirts.
When licks come to an end, tears stay hot.
His father rips up photographs – not porn,
but US movie stars my uncle loves the most –

Clark Gable's beaming smile, shoulders wider
than the house grandfather built – booze-trembling hands,
a roof that leaks, the door half-off its hinges.
He stamps torn photographs in dirt – Cary Grant –
a three-piece suit tight as any hug my uncle wants
to give each god in black and white. As he falls asleep,

these stars are tucked beneath a pillow with no case,
prelude to a life spent loving men. Grandfather
has an eye for boys as well but in a hilltop town,
he has to prove himself, standing underneath the only
lamppost that still works, calling out to passing girls –
*Do you want a drink from my flesh fountain?*

He kneels on Sunday as the priest stands-in for God,
shouts *Sodomites are damned to hell!* If caught,
they're thrown into a jail with a damaged roof –
sun punishing their heads, harder when it rains,
each drop a lash. God means to cleanse them all.
A child resists by cursing at a stream.

## Library of Bats

My uncle scans the room a final time, never mind
a kick aimed at his back, damaging the golden suit –
dapper to the last. He's beaten with such force,
bones crack as five men laugh. They used the night
to hide next to his house, attack the dust-free zone,
velvet-covered chairs, roses in cut glass.

Men gather close, don't wait to catch their breath,
punch a bloody mouth that says, *Yes, queer. Yes, bent.*
As names like these are aimed, my uncle turns his head.
*Leave my books alone*
dies on his lips as every book is flung. They explode,
a shroud that covers him.

The gang move on, kick the back door open, run
along the path, trample morning glories – whisper
*Did we kill the bender?* Turn a corner,
searching out more drink. Underneath his swollen lids,
my uncle is assailed by bats. Scrawny wings
above his head make him the boy he was,

put to work outside the Judge's house – white
palace on a hill above brick shacks. The boy is paid
with food to sweep up leaves, broom twice as tall.
He peers across the lawn where roses stand in rigid rows.
Makes sure the coast is clear before he looks inside
the house. If caught, he'll face a lick. My uncle sees this

one last time – the Judge next to a box, lifts up a flap.
Wings beat against four walls, all lined with books.
Bats cling to spines, wait trembling for the door to close,
swoop down at leather hides to eat the mites. Boy
whispers to the glass *Will Dracula rise up like in a film?*
*I want a house with books.* No father there to shout,
*Nancy boy, you're too soft.* Bats dim the windowpane.

## Resurrection of a Black Man

They stamp you to the floor,
a gang that does not care. You shone
chipped parquet tiles, proud
of your new Jamaican home. Lush
sounds of fireflies weave through
a garden coaxed from damaged soil,
your hands made rife with blood –
red hyacinths next to a field of figs.

One of the tallest trees calls *Father*
at the windowpane as drunken men
kick out. Again, they curse you
to the roof – *Batty man, bye bye* –
voices thick with rum, cracking bones
inside a golden suit you made
to sashay over hills, glide across
blue mountaintops. As men yelled,

*Sodomite* you clicked stacked heels,
hurled *Queer can kiss my neck.*
The same when young and Blighty-bound,
one of the few to swish
from a banana boat, shout
*I'm a bender* to the host, refuse
to doff your cap of fuchsia felt.
My God! You knew the way to strut.

But on this smaller island, sun informs
each bold flick of your wrist. Taken
by the gang as a red rag, they chase
you home, knock down, stamp hard.
What if their feet could be reversed?
Not walking on your spine but forced
beyond flamboyant trees. Wild
jasmine, known to purify, will trip them

in a nettle bush. Pricks shall exorcise
blood lust. The root of hate twists
in the ground. I'll feed you healing plums.
Before your final breath, you'll reach
for juniper as it rejuvenates. What more
can nature do to bring you back?
The gang stamps from your house.
A fig tree calls you *Father*.

## Acknowledgements

Poems in this collection have previously been published by, or in association with, Brighton and Hove Poetry Competition, Butcher's Dog, Cardiff Review, Fosseway Poetry Competition, Gitanjali and Beyond, Magma, The New European, The Interpreter's House, perhappened, Poetry Birmingham, Segora Poetry Competition, Steel Jackdaw, Under the Radar, Versodove.

*Hymn to Jamaica*: Epigraph taken from 'Going Home Rejoicing' by F. Crosby & J. Sweney.

Many thanks to Dawn Bauling, Ronnie Goodyer, Katharine Hoare, Maggie Brookes-Butt and the Crucial Words Poetry Group.

Special thanks to Nancy Christina Downie, Margaret Livinia Mitchell, David Mitchell, Margaret Rose Mitchell, Milton Williams, Joseph Mark Letang and Mark Anthony Mitchell.

Indigo Dreams Publishing Ltd
24, Forest Houses
Cookworthy Moor
Halwill
Beaworthy
Devon
EX21 5UU
www.indigodreamspublishing.com